A STRESSED-OUT GUY'S GUIDE

How to Deal

Travis Clark

JASMINE
HEALTH
Wellness • Diet • Cooking

Jasmine Health, an imprint of Enslow Publishers, Inc.

Library of Congress Cataloging-in-Publication Data

Clark, Travis, 1985-
 [Guys' guide to stress]
 A stressed-out guy's guide : how to deal / Travis Clark.
   pages cm. -- (A guy's guide)
 Originally published in 2008 as the author's A guys' guide to stress.
 Includes bibliographical references and index.
 Summary: "Explores the emotion of stress in young men and the best ways to deal with it and the situations that cause it. Includes real-life examples, quotes, facts, tips, and quizzes"—Provided by publisher.
   ISBN 978-1-62293-010-4—ISBN 978-1-62293-011-1 (pbk) — ISBN 978-1-62293-012-8 (ePUB) — ISBN 978-1-62293-013-5 (PDF) — ISBN 978-1-62293-014-2 (PDF) 1. Stress (Psychology). 2. Boys—Life skills guides. I. Title.
 BF575.S75C545 2014
 155.5'32—dc23
                          2013015760
Future editions:
Paperback ISBN: 978-1-62293-011-1   EPUB ISBN: 978-1-62293-012-8
Single-User PDF ISBN: 978-1-62293-013-5   Multi-User PDF ISBN: 978-1-62293-014-2

Printed in the United States of America
072014 HF Group, North Manchester, IN
10 9 8 7 6 5 4 3 2 1

To Our Readers: We have done our best to make sure all Internet addresses in this book were active and appropriate when we went to press. However, the author and the publisher have no control over and assume no liability for the material available on those Internet sites or on other Web sites they may link to. Any comments or suggestions can be sent by e-mail to comments@enslow.com or to the address below.

Jasmine Health
Box 398, 40 Industrial Road
Berkeley Heights, NJ 07922
USA
www.jasminehealth.com

Illustration Credits: Shutterstock.com: Christos Georghiou (clipboard graphic), 18; Cory Thoman (brain-storm graphic), pp. 16, 19, 31, 50; Dwaschnig, p. 1; freesoulproduction (thumbtack graphic), pp. 5, 6, 7, 9, 11, 15, 21, 26, 39, 48, 51, 52, 53, 56; NLshop (therapist graphic), pp. 22, 23, 24, 25, 30, 34, 35, 38, 42, 43, 46, 47, 56, 60, 61; Seamartini Graphics (atom graphic), pp. 10, 59; vectorgirl (lightbulb graphic), p. 21; zayats-and-zayats (quotation graphic), pp. 10, 14, 18, 27, 54, 60.

Cover Photo: Dwaschnig/Shutterstock.com

This book was originally published in 2008 as *A Guys' Guide to Stress.*

CONTENTS

CHAPTER ONE

Stress and Stressors

It was the night before a huge test, and Philip was over at his friend Tim's house. They had been studying all afternoon for their European History test the next day. Both of them wanted to do well. But there was a lot of material to cover. Even though they studied for several hours, both felt nervous about how they would do.

The feeling that Tim and Philip are dealing with is called stress, which is the body's reaction to an external force or event. In Tim and Philip's case, that outside event is the test they face the next day. The test is their stressor—the term used to describe something that causes stress.

A stressor can be several different things—a project, a job, a large crowd, an illness, an immediate danger, or even hunger, just to name a few. Generally, any type of change in a person's normal routine can cause stress. When stressful situations occur, the body prepares to deal with a challenge or tough situation by increasing alertness and focus. Up until the mid-1930s, the concept of stress did not even exist. Around that time, a physician named Hans Selye first noticed that his patients shared many of the same symptoms, although they suffered from different diseases. These complaints typically involved aches, pains, and nausea.

When Selye investigated the biological causes of the symptoms, he came to the conclusion that something within the body was causing it to react, or adapt, to illness. Through further research Selye learned that the body responded the same way, whether it was reacting to an illness, the injection of foreign bodies, or some other external force. Selye referred to this ability of the body to react and adapt as general adaptation syndrome. He would later call it stress.

Selye's research has led to a greater understanding of how the human mind can cause changes in the human body. He has also helped future generations understand why the body reacts to outside forces in different ways.

Stress can involve many emotions, ranging from excitement to anger, fear, embarrassment, guilt, or shame.

You and Your Emotions

A part of everyone's personality, emotions are a powerful driving force in life. They are hard to define and understand. But what is known is that emotions—which include anger, fear, love, joy, jealousy, and hate—are a normal part of the human system. They are responses to situations and events that trigger bodily changes, motivating you to take some kind of action.

Some studies show that the brain relies more on emotions than on intellect in learning and in making decisions. Being able to identify and understand the emotions in yourself and in others can help you in your relationships with family, friends, and others throughout your life.

Everyone responds to stress differently. Some people may be very bothered by having a major test, while others feel completely confident. On the other hand, the confident test-taker may fall apart when having to give a speech in front of a group of people, while the nervous test-taker can easily speak before the whole student body. Similarly, the amount of stress that people can handle varies from person to person.

While a little bit of stress in your life can help you be at the top of your game, too much stress in life can cause health problems. That's why it's a good idea to learn how to manage stress. You can do this by learning how to identify your stressors and why they make you feel stressed. That way, you can know when it is time to make changes or take action to reduce stress in your life—and keep it from overloading your system.

Common Stressors for Guys

Can you identify with any of these stressors and the emotions they cause?

1. Starting at a new school
2. Trouble with family and friends
3. Overloaded with school work, job, chores
4. Highly competitive athletics
5. Lack of rest
6. Desire to fit in
7. Birth of a new brother or sister
8. Tests or exams
9. Death of a family member or friend
10. Big social event, party, or date
11. Body changes of puberty

CHAPTER TWO

Your Body's Response

> The auditorium was full for the school assembly. The entire high school had filled the 1,000-seat auditorium and the crush of people was really starting to bother Will. He didn't like large crowds but was okay when he could talk with his friends. However, they had decided to skip the assembly, leaving him stranded. As Will looked around the auditorium, he grew more uncomfortable. Waves of nausea began washing over him, and he started to sweat. Unable to bear his feelings any longer, Will stumbled out of the auditorium. He made it to the hall, where he sank to the floor and tried to collect himself.

Because crowded environments bother Will, he responded negatively to the stress of being in the auditorium. He broke into a sweat and felt sick to his stomach. Why was he feeling this way?

Will's body was responding to stress. The physical symptoms can range from a headache, to nausea, to a rash, to an anxiety attack. (An anxiety attack is when you feel overwhelmed by apprehension and fear. Symptoms include sweating, rapid heartbeat, and tension.) Anxiety often involves a number of different emotions, including fear, shame, and sometimes guilt. Feelings of anxiety commonly occur as a result of overstress, which occurs when your body is exposed to a high level of stress.

In his research, Hans Selye examined how the human body physically responds when under stress. He eventually identified an internal stress-causing system, known as the hypothalamus-pituitary-adrenal system. The stress response starts in the brain, where the hypothalamus is located. The hypothalamus directs the pituitary gland, which is also in the brain, to send a message to other organs in the body. As a result certain chemicals, called hormones, are released into the bloodstream.

Classifying Stress

Physical—Headaches, nausea, vomiting, sweaty palms, stomachaches

Emotional—Sadness, worry, fear, anxiety, depression, irritability

Behavioral—Difficulty concentrating, nervousness, daydreaming, nightmares, difficulty sleeping

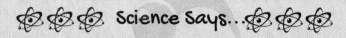

⚛⚛⚛ Science Says... ⚛⚛⚛

Hans Selye theorized that the body goes through three different stages when exposed to stress:

Alarm reaction: This is the body's initial excitement after recognizing the stressor. In a response known as "fight-or-flight," the body prepares to take action. This causes a high level of activity within the body: the muscles tense, blood pressure rises, and the rate of breathing increases.

Resistance: The body begins to deal with the stress. Depending on the stressor, the body will react in various ways. But it is also attempting to move back to normal.

Exhaustion: If the body has to endure a high level of stress for a long period of time, its ability to cope or resist will be worn down. The result can be a weakened immune system and illness.

"Worry and stress affects the circulation, the heart, the glands, the whole nervous system, and profoundly affects heart action."
—Charles W. Mayo

Two hormones that increase in response to stressful situations are adrenaline and cortisol. These stress hormones come from the adrenal glands, which are located on the top of the kidneys. The additional amounts of adrenaline and cortisol cause the amount of sugar in the bloodstream to increase, resulting in a feeling of extra strength and energy. The adrenaline and cortisol can cause many other body changes, including a rapid heartbeat, sweaty hands, and upset stomach.

Physical Symptoms of Stress

headache

aching neck and shoulders

flushed face

teeth grinding

rapid heartbeat

poor appetite

sweaty hands

shaking legs

dry mouth and throat

heartburn

upset stomach or nausea

In Will's case, the stress of being in a hot, crowded room triggered extreme feelings of discomfort, nausea, and nervousness. His response was to remove himself from the environment—that is, to flee from it.

This response to stress is known as the fight-or-flight response. When the body senses danger or some kind of emergency, it prepares either for fighting or for fleeing from attack. The fight-or-flight instinct dates from prehistoric times and helped ensure that early humans could survive in a dangerous world.

Although humans no longer need this survival instinct to fight or escape from wild animals, the automatic reflex remains. The body has the same reaction whenever you are actually facing a dangerous situation or simply catching yourself as you trip on the stairs. Stressful situations as well as emotions such as anger will also trigger the stress response.

CHAPTER THREE

Messed With Stress

> Scott was upset. As he walked home from school, he tried to figure out how he was going to get everything done. He knew that he had to read fifty pages for his American Literature class, study for a biology test, and finish a project that he had been working on for history. On top of all that, in thirty minutes he had to be at a three-hour practice. How in the world would he be able to fit in all the work he had to do?

Scott has a lot on his plate, and he's feeling stressed. Sometimes "achievement overload," a phrase coined by David Elkind in *The Hurried Child: Growing Up Too Fast Too Soon* (2001), can cause kids to feel stressed out (feeling exhausted and physically ill because of overstress). This happens when teens try to include as many activities into their lives as possible.

In addition to carrying a busy school workload, they are trying to balance numerous extracurricular activities—such as dance or music lessons, volunteer work, part-time jobs, and various sports. The pressures

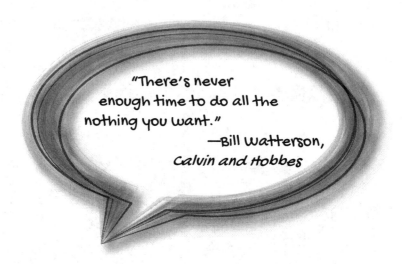

"There's never enough time to do all the nothing you want."

—Bill Watterson, *Calvin and Hobbes*

that come with taking part in so many extracurricular activities can have a negative effect on their health.

Like Scott, you may be trying to do well at school while participating in lots of extracurricular activities. It can be difficult to deal with tests, projects, and other challenges of education without feeling stressed out.

Make a plan. Don't let your schoolwork overwhelm you too much. Pulling all-nighters before a big test or doing nothing but studying will cause even more stress. Set aside time to do your homework, and be sure to give yourself a break every now and then. However, that doesn't mean you should treat academics lightly, because it is important to always try to do your best and to be prepared for school.

The way you respond to the pressures of school can either help you relieve stress or make it worse. In Scott's case, he could simply sit down and figure out the best way to take care of his work that night. For example, maybe he could skip his sports practice. This would be taking a direct action to deal with his stress. Deciding to stick to a plan of getting home from school, taking a short break, and then immediately settling down to work would be another way for Scott to get everything accomplished. By coping with his stress directly, Scott could avoid problems that might occur if he didn't get his work done. Sometimes, not taking immediate action to deal with a busy schedule will lead to even greater stress.

Set priorities. If you are putting too much pressure on yourself to a point where you are feeling overwhelmed, you need to stop and think about whether you are overcommitting yourself. Take a moment to prioritize what is important to you. Think about what you like to do best and put that at the top of your list. You may have to make a hard decision and stop guitar lessons so you can make all the necessary basketball practices. Remember that you need to make time for yourself in order to feel better about yourself.

Remember that stress can affect your health, behavior, thoughts, and feelings.

Stressor Scenarios

The next time you feel stressed out about a situation, keep in mind that there are many different ways you can respond. Which of the following solutions do you think would produce the best results? Which could cause even more stress?

1. **Martin is running for class president. Winning the election is a big deal for his parents, who want to see him succeed at all costs. Martin is uncomfortable with their attitude. What do you think he should do?**

    A. Talk to his parents and let them know that they are putting a lot of pressure on him.

    B. Go all out and spend all available hours of the day preparing for the election. Put posters up all over the school; create buttons and stickers to promote his campaign.

    C. Crumble under the stress and drop out of the election.

2. **John is playing in his first basketball game for the freshman team. He's nervous and becoming stressed out the night before the next game. What should John do?**

    A. Go to school the next day and pretend that nothing is bothering him. Trying to forget it will make it go away, right?

    B. Get to school early the next day and try to shoot the ball around before homeroom. This will give him more confidence and get him excited for the game.

    C. Go to see the coach the next day and quit the team.

3. Mark is failing his class and has to get an "A" on the next test in order to bring up his grade. What's Mark's next move?

A. Work hard every night prior to the test, studying and making flashcards, and get his parents to help him study. Go in to see the teacher for extra help.

B. Watch TV every night instead of studying. Casually flip through the textbook the night before the test.

C. Decide that he is a failure in life and give up.

Answer Key

Question	Less Stress	More Stress
1.	A	B, C
2.	B	A, C
3.	A	B, C

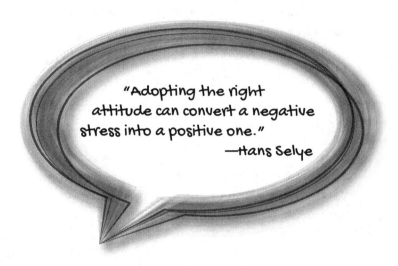

> "Adopting the right attitude can convert a negative stress into a positive one."
>
> —Hans Selye

The Survey Says...

In 2005, Boys and Girls Clubs of America conducted a survey of disadvantaged kids ages thirteen to eighteen years old. Here's what they said caused them the most stress:

37% peer pressure and fitting in

26% school

19% relationships

11% violence

7% other

How Stressed Out Are You?

Count up the number of sentences you agree with. Then evaluate how stressed out you are.

1. I often feel tense or anxious.

2. I frequently have stomachaches.

3. My family often makes me feel upset.

4. I get nervous around people at school.

5. I often get headaches.

6. I have trouble falling asleep at night.

7. I worry about school.

8. When I get nervous, I tend to snack.

9. I have trouble concentrating on one thing because I'm worrying about something else.

10. I have considered using drugs or drinking to relax.

11. I have a full schedule of responsibilities at school and at home.

12. I have trouble finding time to relax.

13. I often feel guilty that I'm not getting all my work done.

6 or more = *stress level quite high*
2 to 5 = *stress level average*
1 or 0 = *stress level below average*

CHAPTER FOUR

Learning to Cope

Drew was trying out for the school soccer team. Even before tryouts started, he knew that making the team was going to be difficult—there was a lot of competition. However, he managed to survive the first two rounds of cuts. Now it was down to just him and two other players.

As Drew tried to sleep the night before final tryouts, he was feeling nervous. He imagined himself making the team (and how great that would be), and he thought about what a big letdown getting cut would be. For the past few weeks, Drew had spent so much time thinking about soccer that he hadn't been able to concentrate on anything else, including his campaign for class senate and the big assignment in English that was due in three days.

Drew's stress is normal. He isn't going through anything out of the ordinary for most student-athletes. However, he needs to figure out a way to deal with everything that is causing him stress.

One way for Drew to reduce feelings of panic or anxiety is for him to focus on the potential positive outcome. A positive outcome in this situation—making

People who are optimistic and think positive thoughts can handle everyday stress better than negative thinkers.

the soccer team, winning a spot on the class senate, and turning in the assignment on time—would boost Drew's confidence. And it would reduce any feelings of stress. If his thoughts focus on a negative outcome—failing to make the team, losing the election, or forgetting to turn in the assignment—it's likely his feelings of stress would increase.

Acute stress and chronic stress. There are two types of stress—acute and chronic. Acute stress occurs when the fight-or-flight response is triggered but quickly resolves, allowing the body to return to normal. Acute stressors include crowded areas, noise, isolation, hunger, immediate danger, or anything that can overload

Acute stress is the immediate reaction to a stressful situation. Chronic stress is stress that builds up when you have to face one stressful situation after another.

Tips for Coping with Stress

Identify and manage your sources of stress. Try to deal with the problem at the beginning. For example, if you are having a conflict with a teammate on your soccer team, think through the issue first. Then, try to come up with a healthy and direct way of resolving the problem.

Follow stress-reducing activities. If schoolwork or studying is causing you a great deal of stress, give yourself a break every hour or two. Try a stress-reducing breathing exercise like the one shown on page 25 or go outside for a short run.

Connect with other people. While friends and family can be the cause of some stress, they also can relieve it. Sometimes you need to hang out and spend time with friends. Go see a movie, hang out, play a sport, and take your mind off what is stressing you out.

After completing a hard task or getting yourself out of a tight spot, reward yourself. Go do something that you truly enjoy and that will help you relax.

you in a short amount of time. These stressors trigger the fight-or-flight response. The heart beats faster, the breathing rate increases, and the blood pressure rises. This is why acute stressors can be dangerous, especially for anyone with heart disease. The sudden increase in blood pressure can cause serious heart trouble.

Chronic stress is stress that is continuous and that accumulates over time. Chronic stressors can include having a large amount of work at school, trying to balance school and job responsibilities, having relationship problems, or feeling lonely or isolated.

With chronic stress, the stress response doesn't shut down. Stress hormone levels in the bloodstream remain high, and that can have a negative effect on the immune system (which protects the body from disease and harmful substances). As the body deals with pressure from long-term stressors, it can become worn down and less able to combat illnesses.

Learn to recognize your stress signals. Like Drew, you may have a lot going on in your life. And your body

Other Ways to Relieve Stress

- Spend some time alone.
- Listen to your favorite music.
- Work on your favorite hobby or start a new one.
- Play a musical instrument.
- Shoot some baskets or join friends in a pickup game.
- Review your commitments and give at least one obligation up.

It's perfectly normal for you to feel stressed, but whenever possible you should try to reduce stress by dealing with its causes in a direct way.

One Way to De-Stress

If you come home from a stressful day at school, try to identify what went wrong. On a piece of paper, write out your feelings by finishing these sentences:

I felt angry when . . .

I felt troubled when . . .

I was offended when . . .

I felt hassled when . . .

I was frustrated when . . .

I got anxious when . . .

This exercise will help you think through why you felt stressed out. When you take time to stop and think about your problems, you can put them in perspective. And evaluating your stress can help you figure out ways to lighten the load you are placing on yourself.

Stress Reducer: Breathing Exercise

When you're under a lot of stress, you breathe rapidly. To help yourself calm down and relax after a stressful experience, try the following exercise:

1. Inhale through your nose slowly and count to ten.

2. As you breathe, expand your stomach and raise up your abdomen, but make sure your chest doesn't rise up.

3. Exhale through your nose completely and slowly, counting to ten.

4. Block out everything else by concentrating on breathing and counting.

5. Repeat five to ten times.

may be telling you that it is stressed out. That knot in your stomach, feelings of irritability, a reoccurring headache, or difficulty concentrating can all be symptoms of chronic stress.

Identify your stressors. Are you bothered because a friend is pressuring you to do something you don't want to do? Are you worried about money? Are you having trouble getting along with your parents, your brother, or your sister? Are you feeling overwhelmed by having too much schoolwork? All of these are stressors that teens have identified in their lives.

Eat a Healthy Diet

According to the U.S. Department of Agriculture, a healthy diet should include an assortment of foods from the following categories:

- **Grains**—particularly whole grains and brown rice.
- **Vegetables**—dark green (such as broccoli and leafy lettuce); orange (such as acorn squash, carrots, and sweet potatoes); starchy (including corn, green peas, and potatoes); and dry beans and peas.
- **Fruits**—any fruit or 100 percent fruit juice.
- **Milk and dairy products**—including low-fat milk and cheeses.
- **Meats**—lean cuts of meats such as beef and pork, as well as fish and shellfish.
- **Oils**—including canola, corn, and olive oil.

For more information, check out the food and nutrition link at the U.S. Department of Agriculture Web site.

Once you can identify the conflict or issue that is causing you stress, you can take steps to do something about it. Try to come up with a way to deal with the situation or change it. For example, if a homework assignment is bothering you, you can talk to the teacher who assigned it. If your kid sister is teasing you all the time, ask her what is really bothering her. If she won't talk, tell her you're planning to let your parents know what's going on if she doesn't stop.

Keep yourself healthy. You will be better able to cope with or reduce stress in your life if you are healthy. Simply following a healthy lifestyle—eating a proper diet and exercising regularly—will help you keep stress levels down.

Eating a healthy diet means eating three meals a day, and sticking with nutritious foods. (See the suggestions for a healthy diet on page 26.) And be aware that certain foods can make stress worse. Among them are caffeine-rich foods such as coffee, certain sodas, and chocolate. Caffeine is a drug that causes a release of adrenaline—and feelings of stress. Other foods to avoid are sugary treats. Although they provide a sudden boost of energy, foods that are high in sugar can wear off quickly and cause irritability and poor concentration.

"Rest is not a matter of doing absolutely nothing. Rest is repair."
—Daniel W. Josselyn

A great stress reliever is exercise. Spending time exercising will not only help you take your mind off your stressors but also relieve any tension building up inside. Make time for an activity you really enjoy and exercise three times a week for at least thirty minutes at a time. Exercise relaxes tense muscles and has a positive effect on mood. That's because when you exercise, your brain releases chemicals called endorphins—natural substances that make you feel good.

Make sure you get enough sleep, too. It's easy to run out of time for something like sleep if you are involved in a lot of activities such as sports and clubs or have responsibilities like a part-time job, house chores, and homework. Regardless, it is important that you figure out a way to budget your time to get at least seven to eight hours of sleep each night. Getting a healthy amount of sleep will help you stay focused and keeps you energized. And that can be especially useful before a big test, game, or other potentially stressful event.

Of course, you do want some stress in life. Otherwise, you might find it hard to motivate yourself or feel a sense of worthiness. But too much stress is a bad thing. What is important is knowing how to manage your stress. You know yourself best and are the only one who can determine what stress you are able to sustain and what stress causes you pain.

CHAPTER FIVE

Unhealthy Ways to Cope

> "I stomp around the house and pound on my brother."
> (Tim, age 15)
>
> "I drink and smoke." (Aaron, age 16)
>
> Earl Hipp, *Fighting Invisible Tigers: A Stress Management Guide for Teens* (1995)

These comments reflect the ways some teenage guys cope with stressful situations. However, their methods for dealing with stress do nothing to fix the problem. In fact, these responses are all harmful. Unfortunately, there are many negative ways in which people deal with stress.

Overreacting and venting. Lashing out at others because you're under stress does nothing to get to the heart of your problem. In fact, the people who are the object of your anger or yelling are likely to respond with similar actions. They're going to yell and scream, too. Overreacting and venting can also lead to violence.

Suppressing, avoiding, or ignoring. Many times, people avoid thinking about their problems as a way to escape from their stress. Others zone out by listening to music. While this can be one way to cope with short-term stress, if you are constantly plugged into your MP3 player, you are avoiding having any contact with others. And those people could be helping you resolve some of your problems.

Abusing harmful substances. Cigarettes and alcohol are two common "quick fixes" that younger people turn to in order to relieve stress. In 2005, the National Institute on Drug Abuse reported that 68 percent of high school seniors had used alcohol in the past year. The report also showed that 23 percent had used cigarettes within the last thirty days. The kids who drank or had a cigarette did not necessarily do so because they were feeling stressed. However, stress probably was a factor in one way or the other.

Don't De-Stress Like This!

Here's a list of what you want to avoid when coping with stress:
- Illegal drugs and alcohol
- Cigarettes
- Excessive amounts of sugar
- Caffeine (coffee or soda)

A Stressed-Out Guy's Guide: How to Deal

How Susceptible to Stress Are You?

Your lifestyle can affect how much stress you can take. How many of the following statements do you agree with?

1. I eat at least one hot, nutritious meal a day.

2. I get seven to eight hours of sleep per day.

3. I exercise hard at least twice a week.

4. I don't use tobacco at all.

5. I am the right weight for my height.

6. I have one or more friends whom I can confide in.

7. I am in good health.

8. I do something for fun at least once a week.

9. I am able to organize my time well.

10. I have an optimistic outlook on life.

The more statements you can agree with, the less likely you are to have problems when dealing with stressful situations.

Some kids use cigarettes and alcohol because they think it helps them relax, slow things down, and forget about whatever is stressing them out. Dealing with your stressors by using alcohol and drugs allows you to artificially calm yourself down. But you run the risk of becoming addicted and essentially are doing nothing to solve your problems. In addition, alcohol use by anyone under the age of twenty-one is illegal, so you also run the risk of getting in trouble with the law. If you use tobacco, alcohol, or other harmful substances to relieve stress, you may become dependent. Addiction is an unhealthy habit and, when developed at an early age, can be hard to break.

Poor eating habits. Another unhealthy way to de-stress (relieve tension) involves using food to take your mind off your stress. However, constant snacking as a way to de-stress can have negative effects. While you may get a temporary boost of energy from a sugary snack, the reaction doesn't last long. The effects will quickly wear off, and you will be right back where you started, and yearning for more.

In some teens, chronic stress can lead to eating disorders. Some turn to overeating, or binging, to deal with their emotions. The resulting weight gain can be unhealthy. Others may lose a great deal of weight because their stress makes them lose the desire to eat.

The quick pick-me-up provided by using alcohol, cigarettes, or sugary foods only masks the symptoms of stress. Their use can lead to a roller coaster of emotions, in which you experience temporary highs, then come back down once the effects wear off.

Learn how to manage your stress level without resorting to these unhealthy methods. By developing healthy habits early on, you will be ready to deal with stress for the rest of your life.

CHAPTER SIX

Stress in the Family

> Kyle's brother Zach is the star player on the high school basketball team. Although he works a part-time job, Zach sill manages to get top grades in all his classes. However, Kyle doesn't play basketball as well as his big brother, and the classwork in his middle school is hard for him at times. Last week, when Kyle brought home his report card, his parents got angry with him, even though he managed to get Bs in all his classes. "Why can't you do as well as Zach?" his mother demanded. Kyle didn't know what to say.

Some of the most important people in life are the members of your family. Your parents, brothers, and sisters often are a huge part of your life. However, like anyone whom you spend a lot of time with, family members can also be great stressors.

Parent pressures. Sometimes, as in Kyle's case, stress can come because you believe your parents expect you to do as well as a high-achieving sibling. If you feel that your parents and family are creating an unhealthy amount of stress for you—for example, they want you to get all As, star on the basketball team, and win a music scholarship—you need to let them know if their expectations are reasonable or unfair.

Be sure to talk about the effect this pressure is having on you. Don't be afraid to talk to your parents

Tips on Talking to Parents and Other Adults

Bring up your issue when the adult has the time to listen. Don't try to talk to your parents when they're busy with something or someone else or rushing out the door. Say, "Is this a good time for you? I have something important to discuss."

Be aware of your body language. Don't roll your eyes, cross your arms, or clench your fists. Look the other person in the eyes and try to remain calm.

Use respectful language. Don't use sarcasm, insults, or put-downs when explaining your point of view. Snapping something like, "That's a stupid reason," will only make the other person angrier.

Be honest. Tell the truth about how you feel or what has happened; your parents and other adults want to trust you.

Listen to the other side of the issue. The adult will be more likely to show you the same respect.

Tips for Getting Along with Brothers and Sisters

Spend some time together. Invite your younger sister to play a board game with you. Ask your older brother to kick the soccer ball around. If you spend a little time together, you'll get to know each other better. And you can better understand what he or she is thinking.

Go out of your way to give your brother or sister a compliment. Positive communication is important in building a strong, healthy relationship.

Show an interest in your sibling's hobbies and interests. Attend his or her sporting events, dance recitals, and other activities and invite your sibling to your games and events.

Pick your battles. If your sibling did something deliberately to hurt you or make you angry, then you need to let him or her know that you are bothered. But try not to lose your cool and get mad if your brother or sister has said something wrong or broken a possession of yours accidentally.

If you find yourself becoming irritated over something your sibling has done, walk away from the situation and take time to cool down. Try to calm yourself down by taking a deep breath and counting to ten. When you can think more calmly, come back and talk things out. Keep your voice low and calm when telling your side of the story.

and explain to them how you are feeling and why. It can make a huge difference and will make you feel good to get your side of the story off your chest.

Sibling conflicts. In other cases, stress can occur because you and your brother or sister simply don't get along. A hostile sibling relationship—with constant fights, complaints, and negative comments—can not only make your life miserable but also stress out everyone else in the family.

Be aware that you can help relieve stress for everyone simply by making the effort to get along with your brother or sister. When a sibling does something to make you upset, don't keep your bitter feelings inside until they escalate into full-fledged conflict. Use a calm, quiet voice to let your brother or sister know that you are bothered. Try talking with him or her so you can work out your differences.

After all, the relationship you have with your brother and sister is unique. You share memories that no one else does. When your brother takes your hockey stick without asking—and you planned to use it that day—or your sister scratches your favorite CD, you have a reason to feel angry. But don't respond to the situation in an unhealthy way. Stay calm, be up-front, and try to solve the issue early on. That way, you'll reduce your own stress as well as that of your parents and siblings.

CHAPTER SEVEN

Peer Pressures

Dave and Anthony are best friends. They have grown up together and lived on the same street their whole lives. When it came time for homecoming, however, they had a little bit of a conflict. Neither of them had dates to the dance, and both had their eyes set on the same girl—their neighbor Lindsey.

One day, while at Anthony's house, Dave brought up the topic. "So dude, did you ask Lindsey to the dance?" he asked. Anthony's nonchalant reply of "Yup" didn't bother Dave too much at the time. But as homecoming came closer, he found he was bothered. After all, he had wanted to take Lindsey to the dance. And Anthony knew that.

Friendships can cause a great deal of stress. The amount varies, depending on the situation. But even little things that friends do can bother you. Maybe your friend took the girl whom you planned ask to a dance. Perhaps he joked with you in a way you didn't like, or maybe he borrowed your basketball and left it at the court. Sometimes little things that cause tension between you and your friends can pile up and stress you out.

Resolving Stress-Causing Conflict with Friends

Friends can cause problems and stress that you don't want to deal with sometimes. It is important, whenever possible, to work out your problems or disagreements. You will become better friends if you make this effort.

- If your friend has said something that upsets you, pull him aside and tell him how you feel. For example, if he is constantly teasing or making fun of you, let him know you don't like it and ask him to stop.

- Make sure that you remain calm when you talk with your friend. If you are feeling bitter or angry, stop for a moment. Take a few deep breaths. This will give you some time to calm down before trying to talk.

- If you think another point of view will help, go to an adult or a friend who will help the two of you solve whatever is causing the conflict.

- Be willing to forgive if the person has wronged you.

Friends can unintentionally do things that make you upset, angry, or disappointed. When you are not honest with them and let them know how you feel about an issue, you will have much more stress than you would if you had been up-front in the first place. It is very important to communicate with your friends—to tell them that you're upset with something they did or didn't do. In the case of Anthony and Dave, it would have been better for both of them if they had talked with each other regarding their shared plans to ask Lindsey to the dance. Having a simple conversation could have reduced the tension—and stress—that Dave was feeling.

Making friends and fitting in. Another stressor for many kids is the search for friends. Most kids in their early teens seek acceptance from their peer group—other kids who share their interests, hobbies, or activities. The stress of trying to make friends can make life extremely

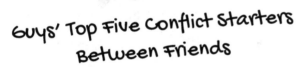

Guys' Top Five Conflict Starters Between Friends

- Who's right and who's wrong
- Bragging
- Who does better at sports or in school
- The rules of games
- Insults and name-calling

Naomi Drew, *The Kids' Guide to Working Out Conflicts: How to Keep Cool, Stay Safe, and Get Along* (2004)

difficult, especially if one person feels rejected or left out of group activities. Kids without friends may often be teased or feel like outcasts.

Sometimes kids develop friendships that create stress. They may hang out with people who really aren't their friends. These so-called friends pick on the other members of their group or constantly put them down.

Stressful friendships can also result when teens experience a lot of peer pressure. Teenagers trying to fit in with the rest of the group or trying to look cool may do things they don't feel comfortable about, such as drinking alcohol or using tobacco products.

The best way to avoid this kind of stress is to choose your friends wisely. Don't settle in with a group of friends who are always mocking you or teasing you. It may be hard to do, but you need to end that kind of "friendship." If a friend is causing you stress by trying to pressure you into doing something you don't want to do, or is simply picking on you, it might be a good idea to spend less time with that person.

While some of your best memories will be of the times spent with good friends, things will not always be perfect. Even with the best of friends there will be occasional bumps in the road. If you find yourself feeling stressed because of friends, try to find a solution to what's bothering you. Be willing to compromise if necessary—but don't stick around with people who cause you more stress then you can take.

CHAPTER EIGHT

School Daze

Day-to-day life at school can get pretty stressful. You may be putting pressure on yourself to earn a spot on the school sports team or in a competitive club. Or you may be feeling stressed out by others. For example, a teacher may have told you that you're not "working to your potential," or you may feel like she's picking on you in class. If you attend a school where you don't feel safe because of the bullying and violent behavior of fellow students, you are being forced to deal with a major stressor.

Dealing with bullies. Bullying can be physical assaults and verbal abuse—or both. You can be pushed, shoved, and threatened. Or you may be called names or have your belongings taken. Someone might be spreading rumors or gossiping about you at school or on the Internet. Regardless of how you are being bullied, the result is the same: you have fear, anxiety, and lots of stress.

If you are a victim of bullying, you first need to recognize that you are not at fault. It is the other person who is behaving in an unacceptable way. No one deserves to be bullied.

Next, you need to figure out some course of action. In some cases, the best way to stop a bully is to confront the person. Don't be afraid to speak out against him, and do not put up with what he is putting you through.

Is Bullying Stressing You Out?

Here are some suggestions to use when faced with a bully:

Take action. Simply ignoring the bully won't make him or her go away.

Go to someone you can trust: a parent, teacher, or friend. Make sure that person is someone you also feel comfortable talking with.

Don't blame yourself for the situation. It's not your fault that you are being picked on. Act confident in situations where you feel bullied—even if you really don't feel confident.

Ask your friends for support. Traveling in a group may help you avoid being confronted by the person who is bullying you.

Find out what your school policy is on bullying. Don't be afraid to report the situation to a teacher.

Test-Taking Tips

As a student, you may find your greatest stressors are tests. Give yourself an extra edge by following these tips:

1. Take careful notes during class.

2. Begin studying early—perhaps a week before.

3. Think up creative ways to quiz yourself, such as flash cards or a jeopardy-type game.

4. Ask your mother, father, or sibling to help you review.

5. Get together with a group of friends to review the material— great minds think alike.

6. Go in and talk to the teacher. He or she might be willing to give you more time for the test—or at least help you understand the information.

The best thing to do is to simply tell the bully to stop. Then calmly walk away. However, if you believe there is a danger of violence from the bully, then you need to tell a teacher, parent, or other trusted adult.

Academic stresses. You may find another major stress at school is the pressure to do well in everything. You may be pressuring yourself to do well on all your tests, or perhaps you're worried about low grades. You may be stressed out with trying to balance outside activities with piles of homework. Or your parents may be placing a lot of pressure on you to get top grades. Bringing home mediocre or even above-average grades can often become a source of conflict in families.

According to researchers at the University of Michigan, one third of U. S. teenagers say that stress is a daily problem for them. Nearly two thirds of respondents to a survey reported feeling stressed out at least once a week. Experts suggest that stressed-out teens try to simplify their lives by identifying the obligations or goals that are most important to them. Then, they should concentrate on accomplishing the priorities. Not only will they do a more effective job, but they will also feel less stressed out.

CHAPTER NINE

The Stress of Change

Pete had gotten used to his parents' constant fighting, although it still upset him a lot. But he never thought his mom and dad would divorce. Soon after his parents separated, Pete found himself becoming more and more stressed out by his relationship with each parent. Because of the joint custody arrangement, he spent two nights a week at his dad's and the rest at his mom's. Pete began to lose track of where he left his schoolwork and where he was supposed to be. Things were spiraling out of control.

Pete's story is just one example of how family problems can be stressful. While his situation is extreme, it is not unusual. Divorce is quite prevalent today. The divorce rate in the United States is 49 percent, and 45 percent of children live in families affected by divorce. It is also common for the mother or father to begin dating again, and the introduction of another adult figure can also cause problems and stress.

Tips for Dealing With Divorce

1. Be honest and up-front with your parents about how you feel about the situation.

2. It's their decision, not yours. Be aware that you will experience feelings of powerlessness and lack of control.

3. Ask your parents to be honest with you throughout the situation.

4. To distract yourself when you're feeling upset, try some healthy stress-relief methods. Exercise, read a book, or phone a friend to talk. Having someone to lean on when times get tough can be a big help. Talking things out are better than stressing out about them.

If your mom and dad have split up and have started to date other people, you have already experienced having to deal with new relationships in your life. Your parent may ask you to approve of the new person or, if he or she remarries, to accept that person as a step-parent. However, you may want to have nothing to do with that person.

The many issues that come with divorce can be hard to deal with. However, by facing them directly, you have a better chance of improving the situation. And you are likely to feel better about yourself as well as toward your family members.

Other family changes. There are many other kinds of events within families that can cause stress. Such family stressors can include the death of a relative, the birth of a new brother or sister, loss of family income when a parent loses a job, or the remarriage of a divorced mother or father. The chronic disease of a family member or friend can also be difficult to deal with.

You may be familiar with the stress of moving to a new community. Moving can be hard, especially if accompanied by simultaneous family changes such as a divorce or lost job. Not only do you lose the friends from your old community, but you are also faced with having to make new friends in a new school.

Making New Friends After a Move

1. Begin a conversation by complimenting a classmate. You might say, "I liked the report you gave today in class," or "That was a great game you played."

2. Ask new acquaintances to tell you about themselves.

3. Share some information about your old school or city, but don't overdo it.

4. Ask about what's going on in your new school and community.

Whether change is positive or negative, it can cause stress.

What can you do? While you can't change the bad things that have happened in your life, your attitude can have a positive effect on what happens next. For example, if your family just moved to a new city, try to think positively about what will happen as a result of the move. Will you live closer to relatives, whom you'll now be able to see more often? Will you be living closer to stores, museums, sports stadiums, or places you'd like to visit more often?

It may be hard, but recognize that with time you'll probably start to feel better about the situation. Give yourself a few weeks to get used to the change, then re-evaluate how you are feeling.

However, don't go it alone. If you're still feeling unhappy and stressed out weeks after a move, talk to somebody. Share your problems with your brother or sister, your parents, or another adult with whom you can easily talk. Sometimes just telling your problems and concerns to someone else can make you feel better. And that person may have some advice that you can try.

As difficult as change can be, it is a normal part of life. You may find that you just need a little time, and your bad situation will turn into a good one.

A Stressed-Out Guy's Guide: How to Deal

CHAPTER TEN

Are You In Over Your Head?

Do you think that you're too stressed out? The amount of stress that you can handle depends on different factors. One of these factors is your genes. That is, the genes you inherited from your parents affect the amount of stress you can handle. If your mom and dad can naturally deal with large amounts of stress, it is likely that you can, too.

Another factor is how much stress you have had to handle in the past. People who have been exposed to some stress when young can deal with it easier later in life because they've learned some coping skills. However, being exposed to extreme stress when young may also increase their sensitivity to it and decrease the amount they can manage.

To get an idea of how well you are handling stress in your life, take the quiz on the next page. A high score may indicate you are feeling the effects of long-term, or chronic, stress that is having a harmful effect on your health.

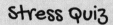

Stress Quiz

Take this quiz to estimate how high your stress level is. For every answer that describes you, add the point value indicated:

1. Are you angry or short-tempered with people?—**1**

2. Do you experience dramatic changes in mood?—**1**

3. Do you feel overwhelmed by schoolwork?—**1**

4. Do you experience frequent muscle twitches?—**1**

5. Are you frequently nauseous or do you have an unusual amount of stomach pain?—**1**

6. Do you feel compelled to do the same routines day in and day out?—**1**

7. Do you constantly feel tired?—**1**

8. Do you feel like you never have time to sit down and relax?—**1**

9. Has a friend or family member passed away in the past year?—**4**

10. Have you started at a new school or job in the past year?—**1**

11. Have your parents been separated or divorced within the past year?—**3**

12. Do you suffer from nagging feelings of guilt?—**1**

13. Have you had a fight with a friend in the past month?—**1**

14. Have you failed a test in the past three months?—**2**

*If your score ranges from **1 to 6**, then you are feeling a low level of stress. A score of **7 to 13** indicates that you are dealing with a moderate amount of stress. If your score is **14 to 20**, you may be dealing with an unhealthy amount of stress.*

Your psychological health. Stress can be a quiet danger in your life, especially when stressors are not quickly resolved. Long-term stress can lead to mental illnesses such as clinical depression or anxiety disorders.

Depression is an emotional problem characterized by strong feelings of sadness and helplessness. Everyone feels sad or depressed from time to time. However, clinical depression is a serious mental health illness characterized by deep unhappiness and feelings of despair. This extreme depression can last for weeks at a time and typically interferes with a person's ability to function in school and at home.

Anxiety is uncertainty toward a future event. It's perfectly normal to feel anxious about day-to-day stressors, such as an upcoming big test, playoff game, or musical performance. However, when feelings of anxiety are excessive, they can be dangerous. In extreme cases of clinical depression and anxiety disorders, people may even come to believe that suicide is the answer to their problems.

Confusion, poor concentration, poor memory, depression, anxiety, and anger are often linked to long-term stress.

If you're feeling troubled by feelings of depression and anxiety, don't ignore them. Get help by talking to a friend, your parents, a school counselor, or another trusted adult. And if you have a friend who seems depressed, be sure to suggest he or she gets support. According to the National Institute of Mental Health, suicide is the third leading cause of death among fifteen- to twenty-five-year-olds. And 86 percent of all teenage suicides are boys.

Signs and Symptoms of Depression

1. Sadness that won't go away
2. Feelings of hopelessness and boredom
3. Feelings of guilt, worthlessness, and helplessness
4. Loss of interest in usual activities
5. Decreased energy and feelings of fatigue
6. Difficulty concentrating and making decisions
7. Changes in eating or sleeping habits
8. Restlessness and irritability
9. Aches and pains that don't get better with treatment
10. Social isolation, poor communication
11. Thoughts about death or suicide

A Stressed-Out Guy's Guide: How to Deal

Top Ten Characteristics of a Highly Stressed Person

If you see any of these characteristics within yourself, you may have a high-stress personality.

1. You overplan each day with a schedule that you must follow.
2. You are always multi-tasking (trying to do several things at once).
3. Your desire to win is extreme.
4. You want nothing more than to advance in whatever position you are in.
5. You can't relax without feeling guilty.
6. When you're delayed, you get very impatient quickly.
7. You commit yourself to too many different activities.
8. You are always hurrying others or yourself.
9. You've forgotten what it's like to have fun for the sake of fun.
10. You are always working, constantly doing schoolwork or your job.

If you see a lot of these characteristics within yourself, you probably have a high-stress personality.

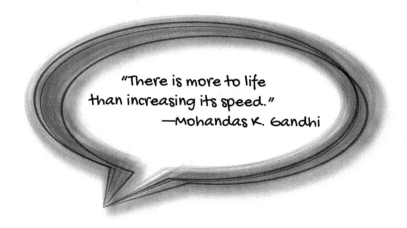

"There is more to life than increasing its speed."
—Mohandas K. Gandhi

Your physical health. Stress has the ability to suck the energy right out of you, making you feel trapped and unable to function properly. The lack of energy and fatigue caused by stress will in turn affect your performance on any athletic teams or in school.

Long-term stress can also lead to health problems that could hurt you both now and in the future. Heart disease and high blood pressure are among the many health issues that have been linked to long-term stress.

Your social relationships. If you let it, feeling overstressed can make your life miserable. Because stress can distract you and keep you from concentrating, it can make learning in school more difficult. When under stress, you are also more likely to become short-tempered with friends, family, teachers, or classmates.

If you are feeling overwhelmed by stress, it is important to take steps to do something about it. Understanding your stress level and limitations will help you figure out when you can handle problems on your own and when you need to turn to others for help.

CHAPTER ELEVEN

When Stress Helps

> *The night before he was to pitch his first baseball game of the season, Bobby couldn't fall asleep. He was really worried about the next day. To try to prepare, he decided to mentally run through how he would approach each batter. At game time, Bobby was ready. He went out and pitched the game of his life, ultimately leading his team to a 9–1 victory. He knew that all his mental preparation had helped him achieve such spectacular results.*

Sometimes stress can be a positive force. If Bobby hadn't been so worried about his game, he might not have been as prepared in dealing with its challenges. In such situations, stress has the potential to be a good thing.

Stress promotes healthy competition and helps people discover new and improved ways for living life. When they get through a difficult situation or impossible challenge, they achieve a sense of pride and accomplishment. In other words, stress can push people to perform beyond their normal expectations.

Even the stress that people typically think of as "negative" can have an upside. For example, controlled or directed anger can help you be assertive—to stand up for something you believe in or that you think is right.

Turning Stress Into Sport Success!

Ever get that stressed-out feeling the night before a big game? Worrying about the game too much will only lead to a poor performance. Here are some tips to reduce and help turn stress into victory.

- Put it all in perspective. It's a game. It's something that you love to play and want to enjoy.

- Concentrate on what you have to do to succeed. Think about throwing the right pitch, making the right shot, or whatever you need to do.

- Keep in mind that you have practiced in preparation for the game. You aren't just going out there having never played the game before.

- Go out and have fun!

If there were no such thing as stress, the world would be a much different place. Without deadlines, would people feel pressed to accomplish their tasks at work? If the outcome of a sporting event didn't matter, would anyone compete? Stress often helps provide the motivation that leads people to accomplish difficult tasks and achieve success.

CHAPTER TWELVE

Managing Your Stress

> Your science project is due today. You want to try out for the basketball team. You just had an argument with your best friend. Your girlfriend is mad at you for forgetting her birthday. Your parents are threatening to ground you for slacking off on schoolwork.

There are countless situations and events—some good and some bad—that can cause stress in your day-to-day life. The way that you manage that stress starts with you. No one else will be able to tell why you are stressing out. Your family and friends may see the outward signs of your stress, such as angry outbursts, occasional stomachaches and headaches, or a lack of ability to concentrate. Although they may be able to guess that you are stressed out about something, they will have no idea about what is bothering you—unless you tell them.

To manage your stress, you need to recognize what is causing it and understand its effect on you. Then take action to deal with whatever is causing your stress—confront and resolve a conflict or lighten your schedule. If you believe you can't handle a stressful situation on your own, you can decide whether or not you want the help of others. Don't be afraid about asking for help if you feel overwhelmed.

Remember, your peers around you will most likely be dealing with similar experiences and the same stressors. By sharing your concerns and problems with them, and learning how they cope with the stresses in their lives, you may get the advice you need.

✺ ✺ ✺ Science Says... ✺ ✺ ✺

According to a 2006 article in *Men's Health Magazine,* talking to yourself could help you feel less stress. The magazine cites a study by University of California researchers in which people lowered stress levels by repeating a key word or phrase. In the study, sixty-six people were trained to associate an expression (for example, the phrase "Take it easy") with relaxing. Then, whenever they felt they were in tense situations, they silently repeated the phrase to themselves. Later, 83 percent of them reported feeling less stressed when using the phrase than when they didn't use the technique.

Where to Go When You Need Help

- Home
- Parent's work
- School (teacher, principal, counselor)
- Minister/clergy
- Mental health helpline
- County social services
- Hotline (See page 63)
- Emergency services

"Nothing can
be more useful . . . than
a determination not to be
hurried. "
—Henry David Thoreau

If that doesn't work, or you aren't comfortable talking about a particular situation with a friend, try talking to one of your parents or another adult you trust. Rather than keeping your problems to yourself, share your feelings with someone else. A parent, school counselor, or other adult may have a different perspective about the situation or have helpful advice. But remember, no

Coping with Stress for Life

Although you will never be able to completely avoid stress, here are some tips that you can use to equip yourself in dealing with stressful situations:

Identify your stressor. If you don't know what is stressing you out, you won't be able to fix it.

Practice the art of patience. Sometimes your stressors will not have quick-fix scenarios. Things will work out if you wait for them.

Prepare for potential problems. When possible, take steps to prevent stressors from occurring. For example, if you are worried about doing poorly in school, talk to your teacher, ask for tutoring, and establish study habits that will help you.

Work hard toward your goals, but be realistic. Keep in mind how much time and effort your goals require, and recognize when you can't accomplish them all. If necessary, cut back on your schedule in order to lighten the amount of stress in your life.

one else can know what is going on in your head unless you tell them.

Stress will always be a part of your life in one way or another. And as you grow older, there will be many obstacles, problems, challenges, and issues that will be put in your path. Some stressors, such as making new friends, will be the same. Future stressors may include having college or job interviews, paying bills when money is tight, or living with roommates.

The habits that you form now to deal with stress you have today will help you deal with stress you encounter tomorrow—and throughout your life. It's up to you to determine the best way to handle your stress and stressors.

Books

Bernstein, Ben. *A Teen's Guide to Success: How to Be Calm, Confident, Focused.* Familius, 2013.

Hipp, Earl. *Fighting Invisible Tigers: Stress Management for Teens.* Minneapolis, Minn.: Free Spirit Publishing, Inc., 2008.

Miller, Allan R. *Living With Stress.* New York: Checkmark Books, 2010.

Internet Addresses

American Academy of Pediatrics: A Teen's Personalized Guide to Managing Stress

http://www.aap.org/stress/buildresstress-teen.htm

TeensHealth: Stress

http://kidshealth.org/teen/your_mind/emotions/stress.html

Hotlines

National Alcoholism and Substance Abuse Information Center Hotline

1-800-784-6776

National Suicide Prevention Lifeline

1-800-273-TALK (8255)

INDEX

A
achievement overload, 13
adrenaline, 11, 27
alarm reaction stage, 10
alcohol, 30–32, 40
anxiety disorders, 8–9, 20, 41, 51–52

B
behavior, 9, 15, 41
breathing exercises, 22, 25
bullies, 41–43

C
change, 4, 45, 48
cigarettes, 30–32
communication, 35, 52
cortisol, 11

D
death, 7, 47, 52
depression, 9, 51–52
diet (eating habits), 26, 32
divorce, 45–46, 50
drugs, 19, 30–32

E
eating disorders, 32
emotions, 5, 6, 7, 9, 12, 32
endorphins, 28
exercise, 22, 28, 31, 46
exhaustion stage, 10

F
family, 6, 7, 19, 22, 33–36, 45–48, 54, 58
fight-or-flight reaction, 10, 12, 21–22
friends, 6, 7, 22, 23, 31, 37–40, 42, 43, 47, 54, 58, 62

G
general adaptation syndrome, 5

H
health, 7, 14, 15, 22, 26, 27–28, 31–32, 49, 51–52, 54
hormones, 9, 11
hypothalamus-pituitary-adrenal system, 9

M
moving, 47, 48

P
parents, 25, 27, 33–34, 36, 44, 46, 48, 50, 52, 61
peer pressure, 18, 37–40
prioritizing, 15, 44

Q
quizzes, 19, 31, 50

R
relationships, 6, 18, 46, 54
resistance stage, 10

S
school, 7, 13, 18, 23, 25, 39, 41–44, 47, 50, 51, 54, 61
Selye, Hans, 5, 9, 10
siblings, 33, 35, 36, 43
sleep, 9, 28, 39, 41
sports, 13, 15, 28, 39, 41
stress
    and behavior, 9, 15
    characteristics of, 53
    coping with, 20–28, 29–32, 58–61
    definition, 4–7
    and emotions, 5, 6, 7, 9
    and hormones, 9, 11
    negative ways of coping, 29–32
    and physical health, 54
    physical symptoms, 8, 9, 10, 11
    positive effects of, 55–57
    and psychological health, 51–53
    signals, 23–25
    stages of, 10
    types, 21–23
stressors, 4, 7, 21–23, 25, 28, 31, 33, 43, 47, 51, 59, 61, 62
    change, 45–48
    family, 33–36
    friends, 37–40
    school, 41–44
stress-reducing activities, 22, 23, 24, 25, 28
suicide, 51–52
surveys, 18, 41

T
test-taking tips, 43

A Stressed-Out Guy's Guide: How to Deal